Songs of Youth, ~~Songs~~ of Death

"Is everybody in?
Is everybody in? ... The ceremony is about to begin"

Death sends you somewhere, more than other things do. It will call out to every edifice of who and what you are - it will surround you and penetrate you. It will lead and it will follow.

Death came to me as a curiosity and developed into an obsession - from a very young age. As the only tangible and seemingly true element of living, it was different; and therefore became the starting point of my inquiry (into what life is), rather than endpoint as it is for so many. I was enthralled by existentialism before I knew what it was. As a child I wondered endlessly about what we were doing with our lives when they were so finite – it drove me insane that no-one seemed to notice. As a teenager when I heard Jim Morrison scream: *'How many of you people know you're alive?',* I felt like this was the first true thing I'd ever heard anyone say.

Later death came to me physically, in my body, when I experienced an aggressive blood cancer. This experience left me feeling very alive. Then, after a seemingly short space of time, my mother chose to die. I no longer felt curious, or fully alive at all. Some other adventure has happened since - and although death is only part of the whole (life), it seems to have dominated large periods of my thinking and being.

My psychological fallout was damning for the ontological reality that presents itself to you as a young westerner, for societal constructs and the games we play, I just never could conform. Philosophically I was almost forced to unravel my way out of the Western god narratives and their complicit underpinning fabrics, things like absolute morality and ego-centrism, I have been implored to look further back (and further forward).

I am unhinged as a believer in (almost) nothing (though I do believe in love of a sort, and Zen of a sort), I am free as I do not follow, I only listen. I do not dictate, nor am I (knowingly) dictated to. I try to allow others to be free too.

Here I am trying to hold onto myself, for your sake as a reader and as a friend. But like an eel, my 'self' which is true only flows, and is composed of multitudes - it cannot be held. I cannot hold myself.

If I can say something which might be real - this above is the reason I write poetry. It is because I cannot hold myself in my own mind. At any time, I am one thing or another. Sometimes, I am on paper.

However much I feel like I let go of, however much I gain, nothing will die with me, and in this sense, I still feel like I have - and I know – nothing at all.

The irony that as a child I fantasised about every aspect of death, and as I have grown it is death which has ended up stifling my ability to think, is not lost on me.

Don't read these poems as a guide, or a map, only as a story that may contain something, but probably doesn't.

Mayora,

I'll wait for you,

And should I fall behind,

Wait for me.

Contents

At the Cliff Edge

I looked to the heavens and vehemently cursed god's
name

As she choked to death in front of my eyes and let go of
my hand

But heaven was a bland ceiling and god was never even
born

Walk

What kind of place are you sitting in now?

Lost your grip on life, but still walking somehow

Still talking somehow

Empty, empty words
Come back at you from the walls

Your shadow your only friend

Even in the darkness, to you, he calls

Sell yourself for wisdom
Better wise and alone

Then sell that too for freedom

Better dead than overgrown

Remember

Are any of these memories
Any part of me
Is it inconsequential
Can pain
Be set free
Is sanity detrimental

Pray for the beautiful moments
The ones you remember

Didn't we reside
In the morning
And at night
Cold but

Huddled, 'round an ember

Single out the phrases
Most deserving of a smile

Anything ever keep you up at night?
Ever stop breathing for a while?

Are any of these memories
Any part of me?
I believe they're more than that

Try to share
And then they're free

And then exhale

And then it's back

Remains

There isn't much left of me now
Only what came back through the door
Left the rest outside
Out there's not safe anymore

For whatever remains
Suppose I should speak
With the little crust of brain
With this body losing sleep

Shadows weigh me down
And fear is back again
I swallow pills and uncertainty
Scared to invite the end

I've been a man of multitude
I've been a friend and a brother
My sickness always there too
It's always been the other

Bravery and cowardice
They shine the same shoe
Friend
You're clueless
If you ever think
Both those men ain't you

Dancing comes to meditate
Like all things do
Meditate long enough

You'll end up dancing
And dead
Just like

All things do

Cry

I miss the way I used to need to tell you stuff
The way you used to listen

There couldn't be another pair of ears for what I had to
say

I'd clamber impatiently to tell you the news

And you'd listen
Because you cared

I've not told anyone much since
I don't believe I forgot

But it's true
I forgot that I used to only want to tell you

How I've grown up

Mum I've grown up so much

I'm nearly 30 now

And I don't have anyone to tell
Not the things I want you to hear
Nothing much in particular

It'd be okay if I had something particular

But I never remembered, not these years, not until now
I just want to sit with you for only a few minutes

Please just listen again

What I did is, I became a man

I got so lucky mum
I don't know how I did it

Can you hear me?

I tried to be kind where I could
I tried to explore
After you were gone

When it just all wrapped itself around me, until I
couldn't breath

I thought I was brave
I thought I was brave

All the time I stopped crying
I thought I wasn't sane

How did I forget that I used to wait all day
To tell you

To watch as you listened

To watch you care
How could I forget, such a simple thing
To ask you a question

It was easier than remembering. I'm ashamed that I
coped. But I forgot to say I love you, because you can't
say it back. And all I want is a couple more minutes, to
tell you about my lunch or that I've got hair on my back.
I want to show you all the things I've seen, tell you the
stories of how I was bold and took on the adventures,
show you the scars. Show you the girl of my dreams.
Just a couple more minutes to tell you, hey, mum,

Hey, mum,

I forgot I need to tell you, I'm all grown up.

I hope I'm doing okay.

I miss you so much every day.

I miss you

So much

Every day

Travel

I am old and you are young, but we share the same floor

Wait, that's wrong

You are old and I am young, but we share the same floor

That's how it sounds

I am young and you are old
Wrinkles in your skin
Scars below
Too
Underneath
With old life wearing thin

I've had new life
Handed to me
A long draw on the pipe

Into the smoke I've come to wander

Heels tapping, through the night

I've got no time
And neither do you

But old man

You're floating

In front of my eyes
You're not veiled
Or frail
Your heart's still drumming, hoping

You come to sit

You don't defy

You are not sad
Nor am I

But younger than me
It's a small life to live

Where we weep for what we see

It's a small price to give

To grow old, to grow, to be

Thrills

Without beginnings or without ends
In a den of freedom which exists to pretend

All alone is sanctuary
To clean the many gods
To petition written laws
To give it all at no cost

Are you ready kid
For the coming wave
It's a hard hitting surf
Clean water turned to blade

Washing over you in seconds
You were born to be unmade

They all want you afraid

Like that sharp sour justice which creeps through the
night
Death is on your doorstep
No wrong
No right

No settlement or strength
Not in this black midst

No help through this confusion
No fucking eternal bliss

You want answers?
Find 'em
In the world of big toys,
Not old ones locked away
New ones, full bore

New ones

Search,
Till your eyes are sore

Who told you there were answers anyway?

It's not a balance
Not Karma
Just a strip-show where you bleed for bills

The other way round - fucking illusory thrills

Sickness

It's my sickness I hide from you
The sickness in my chest
It's coming back around again
Coming to take what's left

The wounds that close
Just scarred over
They never really heal
As much as you can touch the skin
The sickness is still sealed

I've got to die soon
I've got to die again
But I'm afraid
For the first time in a very long time
I'm afraid

It's my sickness I hide from you
The sickness in my chest
It wants to choke me
And I want it to
I want to choke to death

When it's all said and done
You'll remember me how you do
Don't cry because
I was sick
Don't think I didn't love you

It's my sickness I hide from you
The sickness in my chest

It's coming back around again

It's coming to take what's left

Empty

If it makes you feel bad, I suppose it's supposed to
Guilty or sad, there's little you can do

Maybe vomit
or
murder?

Really remember and maybe god can see
But
I don't see the remaining places

Although god may be dead in which case it's just me
Unable to gaze upon the faces

Ask your god where he was or if he knows the truth
Though I don't think he'll tell you,
He's playing games

On the roof

The bastard

Tell him off or even try to reconcile the death
Suppose it was your fault

God where did humans become empty
Where do I start

Rest

Hold my hand
Hold it as hard
As you can

Take whatever you need
And be free

Take whatever you want
From me

Just don't die with me tonight
I'm at your side
We don't need to fight

Hold my hand
And hold it tight
Just don't die with me tonight

See,

I lay here
Only to rest

I think I'm here
Only
To rest

Happiness

As those who are happy
Are without death

We think there is stability

Shrouded in vibrant
Effortless change

The happy
Die flippantly

Bokonon

If you think there is something for us
Carry on down this road
Where it's going
Where I'm going
Only the wise one knows

The story calls out
To a mind
In doubt
While the
Cast profess to grow

In a darkened corner a
Pen scratches paper
and
The words say
'So it goes'

Home

A word to the only one I will ever love

Take me over to where we sleep
Where we hold

Let's not move
Let's grow old

If you can stick around
Then take me home
To that house we'll build
Take me home

I'll be with you
And I'll stay

Take me home,
I think
You

Remember the way

Love

I choose you
Out of all I can see

Even if we'll weep
It's what we'll be

Because as only we can smile
Only we can be so free

I love you
With whoever I am
If I'm not all together
If I don't cry like a man

If we can make it all that way
All the way to the end

Just remember I give you every second
I give you my death
I give you a friend

I love you
With everything I've got
With everything I am
And
With everything I'm not

Afterword

Well done on making it this far. I'm sorry for inflicting so much of myself on you. This journey of mine has been more than I can contain in words, as the cliché goes. I have made my way across continents, I have run for many hours and sat for many more. I have made and lost great friends (though I have made far more than I have lost). I have realised there isn't ever an end, as much as our conditioned minds may crave one.

Losing my mother in the way that I did certainly knocked me into a place I didn't think I was capable of visiting, I guess, the short story is... *this* is life. Be unprepared for the unexpected. Be ready to be surprised. Cherish what you have when you can, lust for the fucking horizon when you need to, sit alone and cry when it's necessary. Don't stop looking for answers. There may be no real answers, but it's usually because the questions are wrong – so, I suppose the accurate dictum would be: don't stop looking for the right questions. This has been useful for me, don't worry if it isn't for you, something else will fit.

There is no magic, not other than the magic you can see and feel. But you can see, and you can feel.

Those of you who are my kin, who are my people, I love you – and I will fight as fiercely and as bravely as I ever have before to **try** with you, for whatever it's worth.

For those who are struggling, know you are not alone.

I always said that on the back-page of my first book would be a dumb-ass picture of me and lord kitty. So, here he is.

Printed in Great Britain
by Amazon